Crafty girl™

MW00514145

cool you

things to make and do

Crafty girl™

cool you

things to make and do

by Jennifer Traig

CHRONICLE BOOKS
SAN FRANCISCO

Library of Congress Cataloging-in-Publication Data available.

ISBN 0-8118-4234-7

Manufactured in China.

Designed and illustrated by Gayle Steinbeigle
Line drawings by Stephanie Sadler

Distributed in Canada by Raincoast Books
9050 Shaughnessy Street
Vancouver, British Columbia V6P 6E5

10 9 8 7 6 5 4 3 2 1

Chronicle Books LLC
85 Second Street
San Francisco, California 94105

www.chroniclebooks.com

**This book is intended as a practical guide to crafting and cooking.
As with any craft or cooking project, it is important that all the
instructions are followed carefully, as failure to do so could result
in injury. Every effort has been made to present the information in
this book in a clear, complete, and accurate manner, however, not
every situation can be anticipated and there can be no substitute
for common sense. Check product labels to make sure that the
materials you use are safe and nontoxic. Be careful when handling
dangerous objects. The authors and Chronicle Books disclaim any
and all liability resulting from injuries or damage caused during the
production or use of the crafts discussed in this book.**

acknowledgments

To Crafty Girls everywhere.

May your glue sticks always glue, your sequins always sparkle, your friendships last forever, and may you always be the best Crafty Girl possible.

table of contents

*D*o you dream about découpage? Do you spend all your allowance on adhesives? Would you rather have a sewing machine than a sports car? No doubt about it: you're a Crafty Girl, and that's a cool thing to be. Maybe you were born with a hot-glue gun in your hand. Or maybe you've got more ideas than skills. Whatever your crafty aptitude, *Crafty Girl: Cool You* is here to help with loads of cool crafty ideas.

Your friends will love these projects as much as you do. Prepare to become very, very popular, because these projects make great gifts. Bathing birthday beauties love getting homemade treasures like Critter-in-the-Middle Soap Treats (page 110) and Bath Biscuits (page 108). Custom-made cosmetics like Candy Gloss (page 36) and Lip Fudge (page 37) are sure to make them smile. And a gift of a sweet-smelling Sweet Dreams Sachet (page 106) makes anyone feel extra-special.

Maybe you need to feel a little special yourself. Crafty Girls know that looking good means loving yourself and treating yourself right. *Crafty Girl: Cool You* has lots of recipes to help you do just that. Give yourself a yummy Butterfingers Hand Treatment (page 30) or a Strawberry Tootsie Scrub (page 32). If you're hungry for a nourishing spa treatment, try Three Square Meals for Your Face (page 25). And if you just need to get away from it all, indulge in an intoxicating Flower Bath (page 28). Ahhhhh.

If it's your room that needs a makeover, we've got lots ideas for that, too. Make yourself a Blossoming Bulletin Board (page 54) or an Illustrated Curtain (page 58). Get that warm and fuzzy feeling from a Fantastic Fur Frame (page 48) or a Fun-Fur Pencil Holder (page 56). Jazz up your bed with a Dazzling Duvet (page 62) and Ribbon-Tie Pillowcases (page 66). Then crawl under the covers and dream of crafts to come.

Or perhaps you're a Crafty Girl who just wants to have crafty fun. *Crafty Girl: Cool You* will show you how to whip up a good time in no time flat. Make like Mata Hari with mysterious Cryptology Crafts (page 94). Banish boredom with Soda Bottle Bowling (page 78). Or foresee your fabulous future with Fortune-Telling Fun (page 91). We see good times ahead in your crafty crystal ball.

There's a world of crafty fun to be had, so let's get started! You probably have half the supplies you need on hand already. The rest are easy to come by. Your first stop is the craft store. Load up on basics like good glue, acrylic paint, ribbon, and pretty paper. Pick up marvelous must-haves like rhinestone, glitter, and fun fur. If you want to make your own makeup or lotions, your next stop is the drugstore, for beauty basics like aloe vera gel and sweet almond oil. Finally, plan on hitting some thrift stores and garage sales for cheap one-of-a-kind treasures to incorporate into your crafty creations.

Ready? Let's get going! But before we begin, a word of caution. Some of these projects require heat, and some require pointy tools. If you're doing anything that involves a stove, a hot-glue gun, or a knife, be sure to have an adult on hand to supervise the proceedings. Keep your supplies out of your eyes and, unless they're edible, out of your mouth. Look for nontoxic materials, and if you're using smelly stuff like paint, solvent, or adhesives, open a window. Take care, and use plenty of caution and common sense.

You craft. You rock. Now craft on, Crafty Girl!

Chapter 1

beautiful you
(and makeup, too!)

suit yourself:
your features

Let us begin by saying that there's no such thing as a feature flaw. So stop hating your wide eyes, your prominent nose, your expansive forehead, your full lips, or your freckles. What makes you different is what makes you beautiful, and nothing is more beautiful than self-confidence. Here's a brief guide to making the most of your fabulous features. You'll find more detailed instructions in the sections that follow.

Forehead

Some people think theirs is too big. Others think it's too small. You could conceal it with bangs, but we say pshaw. Small foreheads are cute and dainty as is. Big, wide ones make you look smart. Accessorize with some stylish glasses and you'll have brainy beauty.

Eyes

Play up your eyes by enhancing their natural shape. If you're lucky enough to have large eyes, frame them with a touch of dark eyeliner. If they're small, bring them out by lining them in a light color. If they're close-set, use shadow to emphasize the outer third of the eye. Beautiful wide-set eyes look nice when shadow emphasizes the inner third.

Nose

Everyone hates her own nose. It's either too long, too short, too pointy, too snub, too wide, or too bumpy. And it's too bad, after all your nose does for you. It allows you to smell flowers and fresh cookies, and it gives you something to rest your shades on. Love your nose! If you can't, you have two options: Draw attention elsewhere, with dramatic lip or eye makeup, or contour it with a mix of foundation colors. But be warned: Contouring is really useful only for photo shoots. In daylight, your nose will just look dirty. If you've got a nose with character, consider yourself lucky. Strong features make you a rare and exotic beauty. We'd much rather be a bird-of-paradise than a boring old daisy.

15

Lips

Lips come in all shapes, and they're all beautiful in their own way. We suggest you stick with the lip line nature gave you and enhance it with a little shine or color. But if you're really dissatisfied with your natural lip shape, remember that dark, matte colors make lips look smaller, and light, glossy colors make them appear bigger. Experiment with different shades until you find one that suits you.

continued on next page

Bone Structure

Your face is perfectly sculpted just the way it is, and most attempts to change it will backfire. But you can highlight what you have with a little subtle blush. If your face is round, apply blush to the inner third of the face. If your face is long, apply blush on the outer third of your face, low, along the bottom of your cheekbone.

Freckles and Moles

We think freckles are just adorable and should be left as is. Lemon juice won't bleach them, and covering them up with thick foundation will only make you look pasty. But if you like, you can tone them down with a light, sheer foundation. Better yet, play them up with a sheer, shimmery powder. As for that beauty mark, it's just that: beautiful. But if you're really bored with it, go ahead and cover it with a dab of concealer. Then, if you like, add a faux Cindy-style mole over your lip or a Marilyn mole on your cheek. It'll be as though your mole has magically moved. Spooky beauty!

Braces

You could keep your mouth shut for the next two years, but sooner or later you may want to eat or say something. So go ahead and smile your sparkly grin with confidence. Make the most of your metal by playing it up with glitter gloss.

The Basic Supplies

[1] Cleanser

Start with a clean slate. Wash your face with cleanser
and cool or warm (not hot!) water every day.

Oily skin: Use an oil-free cleanser. If you're prone to breakouts, get an acne-control formula.

Normal skin: Choose facial soap or a mild cleanser. If this routine starts to dry
your skin out, choose another brand, or just wash once a day. Use an acne-control cleanser if you're prone to breakouts.

Dry skin: You'll need a moisturizing cleanser. If your skin still feels too dry,
or if your skin is extra-sensitive, you may want to wash it only once a day.

[2] Astringent

This potion tones and tightens your pores. It's optional,
but you may find that you like what it does for your skin.
Pour some on a cotton ball and swipe it over your face
after you cleanse.

Oily skin: Astringent is a great product for you. Choose a good one that contains witch hazel or a small amount of alcohol. You might also like tea tree oil.

Normal skin: Use a mild astringent.

Dry skin: Choose an alcohol-free formula, or skip it altogether, especially if you
have sensitive skin.

[3] Moisturizer

After you've painted it up and scrubbed it down, your face
needs a little nourishment. Stick to simple formulas,
especially if you've got sensitive skin—alpha-hydroxy
acids aren't for you. Whichever one you choose, make
sure it has sunscreen of SPF 15 or higher, and wear it
every day. Skip the SPF at night.

continued on next page

Oily skin: You may find you don't need a lot of moisturizer. But you do need sun protection. An oil-free sunscreen is ideal for everyday use. At night, use a light or oil-free moisturizer, especially on dry and delicate spots, like under your eyes.

Normal skin: Choose any simple moisturizer that doesn't irritate your skin. Use it in the morning (don't forget the SPF!) and at night. If you're feeling too greasy, try a different brand, or use it just once a day. You may also want an eye cream for night.

Dry skin: Find a good, rich cream and apply it morning and night. If your skin is sensitive, pick a noncomedogenic formula (that means it won't irritate your skin). At night, you may also want to use an eye cream.

A Word on Zits . . .

You wash, you tone, you do everything right, and you still get the occasional blemish. It happens. We're here to help. The first question: to squeeze or not to squeeze? You know you really, really shouldn't, but it's hard not to when there's an ornery whitehead staring you in the eye. Resist the urge as best you can. Instead, wash that bad boy down with some cleanser and tame it with a swipe of astringent. At this point you can apply acne medication if you like. But be warned: Sometimes this just makes things worse by drying your skin out, so you end up with a pimple *and* flakes. If you do use medication, use the plain kind—the tinted stuff looks fake. Or skip the medication and apply a dab of white toothpaste (it sounds crazy, but it works). Leave it on for 20 minutes or overnight. If you can't bring yourself to use toothpaste, you can try eyedrops (like Visine)—they'll get rid of the redness. Finally, cover it up with a touch of foundation (not cover stick), set it with powder, and try to forget it was ever there.

. . . and a Word on Facial Hair

Facial hair is a fact of life. Every girl has an occasional breakout on whisker ridge. The unibrow, the hairy mole—these things happen. Don't despair. Keep stray hairs at bay with your trusty tweezers. If you're cursed with a lot of wayward wisps, or if you've got a low pain threshold, it's worth investing in a good pair. They'll banish those bad boys with minimal misery. If you're facing a furry upper lip, you have two options: bleaching or waxing. Bleaching creams are available at any drugstore and are easy to use (though you'll want to have an adult around, and be careful: Leave it on too long and you can get a nasty bleach burn). Waxing is effective but can be tricky and messy. We like to leave it to the experts and get it done in a salon.

The Fancy Stuff

Exfoliants

Exfoliants scrub off the dead skin on top to expose the fresh new skin underneath. You shouldn't use them too often, but they're a nice treat every once in a while. Shop around for cleansing grains or scrubs until you find one you like. Or make your own from $1/3$ cup finely ground oatmeal or almond flour, 4 teaspoons honey, and $2 1/2$ tablespoons yogurt. Leave on for 15 minutes. Rinse off with warm water, gently rubbing your face in upward strokes. If you have sensitive skin, you'll want to use only the most gentle formula, or skip it altogether.

Masks

Masks are the most fun skincare product there is. They make you look crazy while they're on and glowing after they're off. Use them whenever you're feeling blah.

Oily skin: Choose a peel mask or a clay mask. Clay masks can be really drying, so be sure to moisturize afterward. You can also make your own mask mixing 1 egg white with the juice from $1/2$ a lemon. Leave on for 15 minutes, then rinse off.

Normal skin: Use a hydrating mask if you're feeling dry, or a peel mask if you're feeling oily. You can make your own peel mask by puréeing a papaya and cooking it over low heat with one packet of gelatin and a splash of water. Let it cool fully before using. Leave on for 15 minutes, then rinse off with warm water.

Dry skin: Choose a nice, rich hydrating mask. You can make your own mixing 1 egg white and 1 tablespoon of honey with 3 tablespoons of powdered milk. Leave it on for 15 minutes, then rinse off.

tingly

toner

This bracing brew is as refreshing as a cold glass of lemonade on a hot summer day. It's astringent, so it's particularly good for oily skin.

You will need:

1 cup witch hazel (in the soap section at the supermarket)

8-ounce decorative bottle with a narrow opening, washed and dried (an empty glass lemon-juice bottle makes a nice touch, but any bottle will do)

15 drops lemon essential oil

Homemade label (optional)

1 foot yellow satin ribbon (optional)

Cotton balls

[1] Pour witch hazel into your decorative bottle. Add essential oil. Cap bottle securely and shake well.

[2] Attach your label and tie the ribbon around the neck for a polished presentation, if you like.

[3] Shake well and swipe toner over your freshly washed face with a cotton ball. Allow to dry while enjoying the delicious lemony fragrance. Feels like sunshine and a cool breeze in a bottle.

Makes 8 ounces.

desert rose
moisturizer

Do your cheeks feel more like the Sahara dunes than dewy petals? Try this easy moisturizer. It's light and oil free, so it's great for oily skin, too.

You will need:

1 cup water

½ cup fresh rose petals (red ones are best, since they turn the brew a lovely pink; consult the gardener before you whack his or her prized American Beauties)

16-ounce bottle with cap, any shape, washed and dried

1 cup liquid glycerin (available at drugstores)

1 tablespoon aloe vera juice (available at health food stores)

Homemade label (optional)

3 small dried red roses with stems (optional)

1 foot red or pink satin ribbon (optional)

[1] In a small saucepan, heat water and rose petals just until boiling. Let the rose water cool, then strain out petals.

[2] Pour rose water into your decorative bottle. Pour in glycerin and aloe vera juice. Cap bottle securely and shake well to blend.

[3] If you like, attach your label, and tie dried roses around the bottle with the satin ribbon.

[4] Store your moisturizer in the refrigerator. It doesn't have any preservatives, so it can go bad within a couple of weeks if you leave it out (if it's refrigerated it should be fine for a month or two; if it starts looking murky or smelling a bit off, toss it). Plus, it will feel nice and cool when you apply it. Shake gently before each use. Smooth some on, avoiding the eye area, whenever your skin feels parched or rough.

Makes about 16 ounces.

glitter glow

Mix your own body glitter in a flash using any glitter you choose. Special evening? Opt for shiny moons and stars. Want to dazzle the beach crowd? Turn your shoulders a glimmering gold. Feeling exotic? Blue-, green-, or rose-colored glitter adds a magical glow to cheeks and temples.

You will need:

2 tablespoons hair gel or body lotion

Fine glitter (available at craft and art supply stores)

Tiny jars, washed and dried (if you're using store-bought lip balm jars, you'll need three or four)

[1] Place gel or lotion in a small bowl. Add glitter and mix until you're satisfied with the sparkle intensity.

[2] Transfer your mixture to tiny jars.

[3] Use your fingers to apply a thin layer of your glitter potion wherever you need to shine.

Makes about 1 ounce.

three square meals for
your face

Your skin gets hungry, too. Give it the nutrition it needs with this all-day meal plan.

Breakfast

This gentle, exfoliating porridge is just right for taking off dead skin cells.

You will need:

2 tablespoons rolled oats

2 tablespoons plain yogurt

2 teaspoons honey

[1] In a small bowl, combine all ingredients and stir until blended.

[2] Apply mixture to face, avoiding the eye area, and rub lightly in an upward, circular motion. Rinse well.

Makes enough for one application.

continued on next page

Lunch

Soothe and smooth your skin with ingredients from the salad bar.

You will need:

½ ripe avocado, peeled

2 slices cucumber

[1] In a small bowl, mash avocado well and apply to face, avoiding the eye area.

[2] Lie back, close your eyes, and place a slice of cucumber over each eyelid. Breathe deeply and think of a tropical island. Let yourself go for at least 15 minutes, until you're cool as a cucumber.

[3] Rinse and go back to your day feeling refreshed.

Makes enough for one application.

Note

Some people are sensitive to the acids in fruits and vegetables, especially avocado. If either the avocado or the cucumber makes your skin itch, sting, or tingle, you're one of them. Remove the offending fruit or vegetable immediately and wash skin well. If it makes you feel bad, it won't make you look good.

Dinner

This nighttime steam treatment gets out the day's grime and tension. It's like a relaxing cup of tea for your face. Get an adult to help with the boiling and pouring of the water, and don't get your face too close to the hot steam.

You will need:

2 cups water

2 herbal tea bags (use peppermint for oily skin, chamomile for dry skin)

Towel

[1] In a saucepan, bring water to a boil and add tea bags. Reduce heat and simmer for five minutes. Remove pan from stove.

[2] Very carefully pour the contents of the pan into a large, heatproof bowl. Test the steam by putting your hand at least 12 inches above the bowl. If it's okay, put your face at least 12 inches above the pan and drape a towel over your head to create a steam tent. Stay in your steam tent until you feel good and relaxed and your skin feels dewy.

[3] Rinse your face with cool water and pat dry.

Makes one steam treatment.

Flower Bath

Why didn't we think of this before?! Picture a rose in full bloom, how delicious it is to breathe in the fragrance, how silky-smooth its petals feel against your cheek. Now imagine feeling that sensation from head to toe. When Aphrodite says she's in the bath, this is what she's talking about.

You will need:

½ cup fresh rose petals

1 tablespoon lavender

2 teaspoons vitamin E oil or liquid glycerin (available at most drugstores)

A splash of rose water or a few drops of lavender or rose essential oil (optional; see page 23 for how to make rose water)

[1] Draw a nice, warm bath. As it's running, add rose petals, lavender, vitamin E oil, and rose water.

[2] Sink in, soak up the heavenly essence of a rose garden in summer, and enjoy.

Makes enough for one bath.

butterfingers
hand treatment

Bust out the baking supplies, cupcake. Sugar and shortening will soften your skin like nobody's business. Who knew?

30

You will need:

2 teaspoons granulated sugar

1 tablespoon solid vegetable shortening

2 small plastic bags

Bowl of warm water (big enough to soak both hands in) or heating pad (optional)

Hand lotion

Vanilla extract (optional)

[1] Over the sink, pour sugar into one palm, then rub it all over your hands for 30 seconds or so. The sugar exfoliates dead, rough skin. Rinse your hands and pat dry.

[2] Coat hands liberally with the vegetable shortening. We know, you feel like you just rubbed fried chicken all over them, but you'll thank us later. Tuck hands into the plastic bags so you don't get everything greasy. If you like, you can rest your bagged hands in a bowl of warm (not hot) water or under a warm (not hot) heating pad. Leave shortening on for 10 minutes or so.

[3] Rinse off shortening and pat dry. Smooth on some hand lotion. Then, dab a little vanilla extract on the inside of each wrist. You'll smell as soft and sweet as you feel.

Makes one treatment.

strawberry

tootsie scrub

This easy exfoliant gives new meaning to the phrase "toe jam," and it feels fantastic. The fruit acids soften calluses and rough skin, leaving your feet feeling soft, supple, and ready for warm socks, strappy sandals, or the next step in a full-treatment pedicure.

You will need:

2 tablespoons oil (olive oil is best)

2 teaspoons coarse salt

8 fresh strawberries

Foot brush (optional; some body-care shops carry these)

Hand and body lotion

[1] In a medium-size mixing bowl, stir together oil and salt. Add strawberries. Mash everything together with a fork until the mixture is blended but still somewhat chunky.

[2] Rub the strawberry mixture onto your feet with a foot brush or your hands. Work it around in circles on your heels and other high-impact zones.

[3] Jump in the shower and rinse the mixture off. Rub in some lotion and put socks on those puppies to keep the healing moisture in.

Makes one treatment.

personal

polish

Color chemistry is easy. With some white nail polish as a base and eye shadow in any color, you can make custom-colored nail polish to match all your favorite outfits. Unless, of course, your favorite outfit is plaid.

You will need:

Eye shadow in your color of choice

Paper envelope

Bottle of white nail polish

[1] Crumble some or all of the eye shadow into the envelope. Crush it into a fine powder.

[2] Snip a corner off the envelope to make a tiny funnel. Open the nail polish bottle and slowly add the eye shadow powder to the polish, stirring with the applicator brush until you reach the desired color. You may need to cap the bottle and shake, shake, shake to get everything blended together.

[3] Paint those paws and let dry.

Makes one bottle of polish.

Note

If you want only a little polish, you can whip up a mini-batch in a waxed paper cup, but you'll have to work fast, because it dries quickly. Prepare your eye shadow powder (see step 1) and have your nails clean and ready to paint *before* you pour the white polish into the cup.

lemon soft	shimmer pink	suave mauve
orchid	ramp	sunshine
ice	sky	grass

candy gloss

This delicious gloss looks and smells just like hard candy. The only tough part is picking a flavor: cherry, orange, lemon, or lime? Go ahead and make all four. It's like candy without the cavities, but don't eat it!

You will need:

2 teaspoons cosmetic-grade beeswax, finely grated (available at health food and craft stores)

2 tablespoons oil (sweet almond oil is best, but any kind will do)

1 teaspoon tint (use red or orange lipstick for cherry or orange, or finely crushed yellow or green powder eyeshadow for lemon or lime)

1 teaspoon honey

A few drops essential oil (use cherry, orange, lemon, or lime)

1 to 2 clean, dry containers (use recycled lip gloss containers or film canisters)

[1] In a small saucepan, combine the beeswax, oil, and lipstick (if using) over low heat, stirring until melted. Remove from the heat. Mix in the honey.

[2] After the mixture has cooled a bit, stir in the essential oil and eyeshadow (if using) and mix well. Cool a bit more, then transfer to the containers and allow to set.

Makes about 1½ ounces

lip fudge

You love putting chocolate in your mouth. Now you can put it on your mouth. This irresistible lip gloss smells just like chocolate fudge, and it will make you look yummy, too. It gives new meaning to a "chocolate kiss."

You will need:

1 ounce cocoa butter (available in drugstores)

1½ tablespoons solid vegetable shortening

2 teaspoons cosmetic-grade beeswax, finely grated (available at health food and craft stores)

½ teaspoon vitamin E oil (optional)

10 chocolate chips

2 to 3 clean, dry containers (use recycled lip gloss containers or film canisters)

[1] Combine the cocoa butter, shortening, beeswax, vitamin E oil, and chocolate chips in a small glass bowl. Microwave for about 60 seconds, until melted.

[2] Give the mixture a quick stir to blend. Transfer to the small containers. Allow to cool. If you get impatient, you can stick it in the fridge. Once it's set, you can use it. You'll be tempted to eat it, but don't: It only smells edible and is sure to make you sick. Nibble on extra chocolate chips instead.

Makes about 2 ounces

clean teen

This is your basic face, great for everyday and casual occasions. Done right, no one will know you're wearing makeup—they'll just think you're naturally this gorgeous. Some girls have all the luck.

You will need:

Blush (choose cream, gel, or powder form)

Loose or pressed powder

Brow gel and comb or hair gel and an old toothbrush

Neutral eyeshadow (optional)

Eyelash curler (optional)

Mascara

Lip liner in a shade that matches your natural lip color (optional)

Clear gloss or balm

[1] Your first assignment: Smile! This will help you find the apples of your cheeks, the firm, fleshy part that's most prominent when you're grinning. Apply a little blush to them, being sure to blend well. (If you're using powder blush, apply it after you've dusted on the powder in step 2.) Powder and cream blush are the easiest to blend. Gel blush is trickier but gives you fabulous color. Practice getting it on right, and make an honest friend promise to tell you if you look clownish.

[2] Set your makeup and smooth out your complexion with a dusting of loose or pressed powder.

[3] Comb your brows upward and outward and set them in place with brow gel. A little hair gel on an old toothbrush works just as well.

[4] If you like, you can apply a tiny bit of neutral eyeshadow. Cover the entire lid but not the brow bone area.

[5] Curl your eyelashes with an eyelash curler if you like. Brush on a light coat of mascara.

[6] Fill in your lips with lip liner to even out their color. Skip this step if your lips are looking pretty good to begin with.

[7] Finish with a little swipe of clear gloss or balm for just a hint of shine.

freckle face

We're sure you've been teased about them every day of your young life. Take comfort: People only tease because they're jealous. You've been blessed with hundreds of beauty marks and fantastic coloring. Go ahead and show your spots. Here's a makeup treatment that will highlight them instead of hiding them.

You will need:

Skin-brightening moisturizer (optional)

Pale pink blush

Loose or pressed powder

Eyelash curler (optional)

Mascara (choose clear or a light brown unless you have very dark hair)

Brownish pink lip gloss or sheer lipstick (if you have black or dark brown hair, a rose or berry color might be better)

[1] If you like, prep your skin by applying skin-brightening moisturizer.

[2] Apply a little blush to the apples of your cheeks, being sure to blend well. If you're using powder blush, apply it after step 3.

[3] Set your makeup and smooth out your complexion with a dusting of loose or pressed powder. This look is all about letting your natural beauty shine through, so you may want to run a cotton ball over your face to pick up the excess powder.

[4] Curl your eyelashes with an eyelash curler if you like. Brush on a coat of mascara.

[5] Finish with a little lip gloss or sheer lipstick.

healthy glow

Flowers wake up fresh and dewy. People, unfortunately, wake up dull and pasty. Happily, people have makeup. Here's a look that will highlight your features with a subtle shine. Fresh as a daisy!

You will need:

Moisturizer

Iridescent foundation or powder and a big brush

Makeup sponge (optional)

Gel blush (optional)

Eyelash curler (optional)

Mascara

Shiny lip gloss

[1] Apply moisturizer to hydrate your skin. If you're using iridescent foundation, skip this step.

[2] If you're using iridescent foundation, mix it with a little moisturizer to make it sheerer, then apply it to your face using a makeup sponge or your fingers. If you're using iridescent powder, sweep it over your face with a big brush. Concentrate on features you want to highlight, like your forehead or chin. For all-over shimmer, brush some on your neck, collarbones, and shoulders as well.

[3] Apply a little gel blush to the apples of your cheeks if you like. Be sure to blend well.

[4] Curl your eyelashes with an eyelash curler if you like. Brush on a coat of mascara.

[5] Finish with a coat of shiny lip gloss.

in the pink

Marshmallow bunnies, bubble gum, plastic flamingos—all of our favorite things are pink. No color is as fun or as flattering. Pink lights up your face with the flush of health. Here's a look that's pink perfection.

You will need:

Pink blush

Loose or pressed powder

Pale pink eyeshadow (optional)

Eyelash curler (optional)

Mascara

Lip liner in a shade that matches your natural lip color (optional)

Pink gloss or sheer lipstick

[1] Get your blush and paint yourself pink! Apply a rosy glow to the apples of your cheeks. Add a hint of pink color to your temples, your chin, or anywhere else. Concentrate on the features you want to draw attention to. If you're using powder blush, do this step after step 2.

[2] Set your makeup and smooth out your complexion with a dusting of loose or pressed powder.

[3] If you like, you can apply the tiniest bit of pink eyeshadow to the eyelid, stopping short of the brow bone area. You don't want to look wall-to-wall pink, but a little shadow can't hurt.

[4] Curl your eyelashes with an eyelash curler if you like. Brush on a light coat of mascara.

[5] Give yourself a rosebud mouth with a coat of pink gloss or sheer lipstick. If you like, use the lip liner to define the shape of your mouth first. Perfect!

stardust

cinderella

vanity

sunburn

hot pants

villain

Chapter 2

home, crafty home

fantastic
fur frame

Fun fake-fur trim makes a fuzzy frame for your most adorable portraits. Check out a fabric store for colorful remnants of fluffy furs. Don't hold back—decadence is the word. This recipe can be adjusted for any size frame.

You will need:

2 rectangles of fun-fur trim, each 1 by 10 inches

2 rectangles of fun-fur trim, each 1 by 12 inches

8-by-10-inch store-bought frame, with 1-inch-wide border

Scissors

Hot-glue gun or good craft glue, such as Aleene's Tacky Glue

[1] You'll need to angle the ends of your four pieces of fur so that they match up at the corners of the frame (if you know that's called *mitering* you've just scored big points). Just trim the ends of each strip at a 45-degree angle (if you know you're trimming off an isosceles triangle you've just scored big points again). Don't fret if it's not perfect—the fur will forgive a few flaws. Consult the diagram below for extra guidance.

[2] Glue strips to frame, following the diagram.

[3] Lay frame flat until glue is thoroughly dry.

magnetic

personality

You already spend plenty of time in front of the refrigerator; why not stick around there 24-7? Attach a picture of yourself to some magnetic backing, and everyone will be attracted to you.

You will need:

Scissors

A photo of yourself (either full-length or just your face works best)

Ballpoint pen

Adhesive magnet sheets (available at craft and home stores)

[1] Carefully cut out your silhouette.

[2] With the pen, trace the shape you've just cut onto the adhesive backing of the magnet sheet, then cut out.

[3] Peel adhesive backing away, then very carefully match up the cutout photo to the cutout magnet. When photo is positioned just right, press down firmly to seal. Then go stick your magnetic alter ego on the fridge—or on your best friend's locker.

the illustrated
story of you

Make yourself and your friends the stars of your own best-seller. Compile your favorite photographs and stories into a mini-album, then make color copies at a copy shop—one for each of your friends. You can write about places you've gone together, adventures, dreams for the future, or you can make up silly captions. Take a camera on a bike ride or to a big game, party, sleepover, field trip, or other outing. Then use the photographs to illustrate your account of the event. To reproduce this book for a friend, you can use a home scanner and color printer, or a color copier at your local copy center.

You will need:

Glue stick

Photographs

Paper, assorted colors but same size, 10 or more sheets (8½ by 11 inches works well)

Computer and printer, typewriter, or pen

Colored markers, watercolor paints, crayons, etc.

Assorted decorations: ticket stubs, pressed flowers, magazine pictures, whatever

2 pieces of card stock (stiffer paper) for front and back cover (same size as colored paper)

3-hole punch

3 lengths of ribbon, each 1 foot long

continued on next page

[1] Glue your favorite photos to sheets of colored paper. Type or write captions or stories, cut them out, and glue them on. If your story is longer than a few sentences, give it its own page opposite the photograph (or photographs). On every page, be sure to leave a margin along the top or left side, which is wide enough to accommodate a three-hole punch binding.

[2] Decorate with colored pens, stickers, or whatever you like. Decorate on one side only, so pictures won't bleed through. You might want to cut out a paper frame and glue it over your favorite photo. If you have souvenirs such as ticket stubs, wrappers, leaves, pressed flowers, or anything else of a more-or-less flat nature, add them. Here are some fun variations on photo enhancements. Try these:

- Glue on comic-strip speech or thought bubbles.
- Cut out the people in your photos and paste them onto magazine pictures of exotic destinations such as Tahiti, the Eiffel Tower, the Grand Canyon, the top of Mount Everest, or the ocean floor.
- Add magazine pictures of your favorite stars to group photos of your friends for a brush with fame.
- Add wings and a halo to your angelic friends, and a crown and scepter to your regal ones. Or give your pal a tattoo heart inscribed with your name.

[3] Make back-to-back color photocopies of your pages, or scan and print pages out in color. Run out a few pages as a test to be sure that the paper is thick enough for two-sided copies. If paper isn't opaque enough, one side can bleed onto the other. Photocopy, or scan and print, the back and front cover images on card stock.

[4] Arrange pages in order between the covers. Then three-hole-punch the lined-up margins. Fasten with pretty ribbon and tie in a bow.

blossoming
bulletin board

Do laundry. Finish history report. Give dog a bath. Roll eyes and sigh. Nobody likes tackling a to-do list, but tacking it up on a really snazzy bulletin board can make those chores a little more appealing. This beautiful board is adorned with artificial grass and silk flowers. It will make any to-do list look like a day in the park.

You will need:

Good craft glue, such as Aleene's Tacky Glue

16-by-20-inch cork bulletin board

16-by-20-inch piece of artificial grass (available at hardware stores)

10 silk flowers

10 straight pins

[1] Spread lots of glue all over the cork surface of your bulletin board and the back of the artificial grass. Place the grass on the bulletin board, pressing down to get it to stick.

[2] Let the glue dry. You will probably need to place some weights on the artificial grass to keep it flat. Try to choose heavy, small things that won't leave funny crushed patterns in it.

[3] While the glue is drying, you can make your flower pushpins. Snap a silk flower off its stem. It should pop off easily. Then carefully push a pin all the way through the center of the flower. A thimble might make this easier. Repeat with the rest of the flowers.

[4] Use the flower pins to secure pictures, notes, and goals to the grass-covered board. Then cross "Make fabulous bulletin board" off your to-do list.

fun-fur
pencil holder

You will need:

Tape measure

Empty, clean soup can

Scissors

Swatch of fun fur, big enough to fit around can

Hot-glue gun or good craft glue, such as Aleene's Tacky Glue

2 rubber bands

[1] Using tape measure, measure height and circumference of can. Cut a rectangle of fun fur to the same dimensions.

[2] Glue fur around can. Secure with rubber bands while glue dries.

Note Use any leftover fun fur to fuzz out the spine or cover of your journal, binder, or day planner.

summer-of-love
wastebasket

Peace, love, and acceptance come much more easily when your wastebasket says flower power. And it only takes an instant!

You will need:

12 (or more) silk or plastic flowers (the more, the merrier)

Wire-mesh wastebasket

Satin ribbon (optional)

[1] Trim flower stems to about 4 inches.

[2] Push stems through holes in wastebasket. Weave each stem in and out a few times to make sure that it will stay. If you plan to decorate only the top of your basket, weave the stems through the mesh horizontally and cover them with more flowers, so the stems don't show. If you're covering the entire wastebasket, start from the top and work your way down.

[3] For added color, weave horizontal lines of satin ribbon in and out of the wire mesh. Tie in bows to secure ends.

illustrated
curtain

There's no reason you can't have a spectacular view even when your curtain is drawn. Replace your humdrum curtains with a collaged curtain that gives you loads to look at. Peruse old magazines for a fashion, fitness, or travel motif. If you're a skateboard or surfing fanatic, use magazine pictures of your dream rides and maneuvers. Or grab a horse, cat, or dog magazine for a window full of furry friends. If you're inspired, use your own drawings and paintings.

You will need:

Glue

Approximately 54 magazine pages (so start tearing out the cool ones now)

Construction paper in various colors

Transparent shower curtain

Scissors

Clear tape

[1] Glue magazine photos or original art to construction paper.

[2] Lay the shower curtain face down on the floor. If necessary, trim curtain to fit the dimensions of your window.

[3] Tape art panels securely face down, until the whole curtain is covered.

[4] Decide whether you want the cool side to face in or out, then hang your crazy curtain on your existing curtain rod.

make a
switch

Walls are for art and not for anything plain, beige, or plastic. Enlighten your old, plastic light-switch plate with a collage of decadent bohemian artifacts. A handful of flat-back gems, some winsome clippings from the latest edition of your favorite magazine, and a bit of gold paint will make your switch pasha-perfect.

You will need:

Light-switch plate (see step 1)

Assorted decorating supplies: acrylic paints, nontoxic metallic paints (such as Ceramcoat Gleams), flat-back gems, photographs, magazine clippings, and scraps of velvet ribbon

Hot-glue gun or good craft glue, such as Aleene's Tacky Glue

Découpage medium

[1] After an adult removes the switch plate from the wall, make sure it is clean and dry.

[2] Decorate in any way you like, using whatever materials you can find. Go literary and add a snip of paper with a quote from an illuminating book or good ol' Will Shakespeare ("What light through yonder window breaks?"). For an ultra-luxe bohemian effect, glue on a smattering of pictures cut from magazines, then brush with several coats of découpage medium. When completely dry, glue on a border of flat-back gems. Add beads, ribbon, or swirls of metallic paint.

[3] Allow to dry. Get an adult to reaffix the switch plate to the wall.

[4] On. Off. On. Off. On. Off.

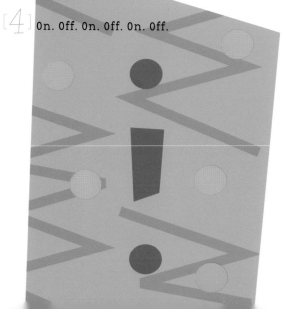

dazzling
duvet

Does your bedding make you yawn? Wake up that tired old comforter with some snazzy do-it-yourself decorations. Check out our ideas or dream up some of your own.

You will need:

Freshly laundered, old or store-bought duvet (solid colors look best)

Scissors

Assorted decorating supplies: felt, pom-pom trim, plastic insects and flowers, beads, fake pearls and gems, ribbon, silk, lace, rickrack, whatever

Needle and thread

Fabric glue (optional)

Note

If you can't find a store-bought duvet you like (or can afford), make your own by sewing together two flat sheets along the sides and top. Stitch some Velcro along the bottom edges for easy opening.

[1] Get your duvet and your doodads and do it up! (If you're using the duvet currently adorning your bed, remove the comforter before proceeding.) Here are some decorating ideas:

South-of-the-Border Bed

Cut cactus and sombrero shapes from felt. Stitch onto your duvet or secure with fabric glue. (When you are sewing decorations onto your duvet, be careful to not stitch through the top to the bottom.) Glue or stitch on a border of pom-pom trim.

Bed Bugs

Stitch plastic dragonflies, butterflies, or colorful beetles around the edges of your duvet. Let one or two adventurous critters head for the center.

continued on next page

Flower Bed

Stitch on silk flowers. Flat flowers such as daisies work well.

Jewel Box Bed

Sew beads onto your duvet. Try pearl polka dots or a random sprinkling of big sparkly gems. If your beads don't have holes, glue them to the duvet with fabric glue.

Moon and Stars

Cut moon and star shapes from felt. Stitch onto your duvet or secure with fabric glue. This motif looks great on a dark-blue duvet. For an extra-special tableau, use glow-in-the-dark stars (craft stores sell these).

 Crazy Quilt

Anything goes. Sew or glue on strips of ribbon, lace, or rickrack trim. Stitch on special beads and patches of pretty silk. If you're really crafty, embroider flowers, dragonflies, or your name.

Pocket Pastiche

Cut 8-inch squares of felt. Sew onto duvet to form pockets. Tuck your favorite stuffed animals or other treasures inside.

[2] When your duvet is all decorated and the glue is all dry, stuff your old comforter back inside and crawl under the covers for a well-dressed catnap.

ribbon-tie
pillowcases

A girl shouldn't have to face unadorned pillows every night. Go out and find yourself a four-foot piece of beautiful ribbon and remedy the situation right now—you don't even need a sewing machine. Nice, wide, washable ribbon that looks sharp on both sides is the ticket.

You will need:

Scissors

4 feet satin ribbon (1 inch or wider works best)

Clear nail polish

Ruler

Straight pins

Pillowcase

Needle and thread

[1] Cut ribbon into four pieces, each one foot long. Cut one end of each piece into an inverted V-shape to prevent fraying. Seal the ends with clear nail polish and allow to dry.

[2] Fold square end of ribbon under 1 inch and pin to open edge of the pillowcase, about 4 inches in from the edge. Pin the second ribbon in place on the opposite side of the opening. Sew each in place.

[3] Repeat with remaining two pieces of ribbon on the other end of the pillowcase opening, 4 inches from the edge.

[4] Put pillow inside and tie ribbons into lovely bows.

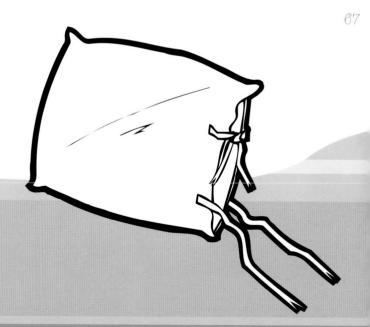

the fairest of them all
fairy-tale mirror

Mirror, mirror, on the wall, who's the craftiest of them all? You are, crafty mama, and this marvelous mirror will let everyone know it. It's decorated with an outline of your favorite role model to let you see yourself in her place. Add some empowering sayings and you'll have a mirror that reflects how cool you really are.

You will need:

Small wall mirror with an unfinished wood frame (available at craft stores or large department stores. The ideal mirror will have a big blank frame to paint on.)

Pencil

Acrylic paint

Paintbrushes in a variety of sizes

Clear varnish (pick one that's specifically made to use with acrylic paint, available at craft stores)

1. Start by sketching your design onto the frame of your mirror in pencil. No need to include a face; your own face will be there when you look in the mirror. Just draw the neck and shoulders, the sides of the face, the hair, and any identifying accessories (like a tiara for Holly Golightly, a gold headband for Wonder Woman, etc).

2. Fill in your design using the acrylic paint.

3. Paint an inspiring caption, like "You look fabulous" or "All Hail the Queen."

4. When the paint is completely dry, brush on a coat of clear varnish.

floating-flowers
paper lantern

The translucent white of an elegant paper lantern sets off your painted flowers in classic Japanese style. Make your lantern as simple or as elaborate as you wish. Even a few small, pink blossoms on a field of white makes for a serenely beautiful addition to your decor.

You will need:

Nonflammable acrylic paint or watercolors and a small paintbrush

Paper lantern (any size will do; look for one at your local hardware store or world market)

Good craft glue, such as Aleene's Tacky Glue

Assorted decorating supplies: mini-mirrors, sequins, and flat-back beads

Needle and thread

Round beads and a charm

[1] Paint a pretty flower pattern on your lantern. Daisies and vines are easy, or try petally pink cherry blossoms. Lotus blossoms are also fairly easy to paint. Look around the house, in the dictionary (under flower names), or at the library for simple flower motifs to copy. Add a butterfly or two.

[2] Glue on mini-mirrors, sequins, and beads to accent your painting. Allow to dry.

[3] String a charm or bright-colored button and 5 or 6 inches of beads on thread. Tie to bottom of lantern.

disco ball

Dance the night away every day under your own disco ball. You'll feel the fever when you see the sparks fly off this glittery orb fashioned from ordinary materials. Change the regular lightbulb in an overhead light or lamp for a red or blue one, and suddenly your room is a disco sensation.

You will need:

Styrofoam ball (8-inch diameter or bigger)

Acrylic craft paint (silver or any color)

Sponge brush

Good craft glue, such as Aleene's Tacky Glue

Assorted decorating supplies: mini-mirrors, sequins, glitter, flat-back gems, whatever

Screw hook

1 yard fishing line or strong thread

Pushpin for hanging (optional)

Blue or red lightbulb (optional— for ambiance)

[1] Paint Styrofoam ball using sponge brush. Add more coats until it looks classy. Allow to dry.

[2] Deck it out! Glue mini-mirrors, sequins, glitter, or flat-back gems all over it in swirl, zigzag, stripe, or curlicue patterns. You can't stop decorating until you drop!

[3] Screw hook into the top of the ball. You may want to brush the hook with glue first to make it more secure. Let dry.

[4] String fishing line or strong thread through hook and knot ends securely. Hang from ceiling by a pushpin or attach to an overhead light fixture.

[5] Install blue or red lightbulbs in your lamp or light fixture and let the dancing begin!

Chapter 3

it's all fun and games

twist and shout

You love having an excuse to (gently) plant an elbow in your brother's nose, and now you do. Play a round of Twist and Shout! Whose knee is in my back?

You will need:

2 pieces of white construction paper, each 8½ by 11 inches, cut into eighths

Markers

2 bowls

6 pieces of green construction paper

6 pieces of red construction paper

6 pieces of yellow construction paper

6 pieces of blue construction paper

red

[1] Get your 16 little pieces of white construction paper. Write "red," "yellow," "green," and "blue" on 4 of them and place them in a bowl. On the remaining 12 slips, write the names of body parts. You'll want right foot, left foot, right hand, left hand, of course, but you should get as crazy and creative as you want to be. Right ear! Belly button! Big left toe! Right funny bone! Put these 12 slips in the other bowl.

yellow

[2] Scatter the sheets of colored construction paper on the floor. You want them close enough so it will be possible to reach red with your left pinky while you've got your right knee on blue, but not so close that it will be easy.

[3] Designate a caller, and you're ready to play. The caller will pick 1 slip from the body part bowl and 1 slip from the color bowl and read them aloud together: "Nose on yellow!" All players must then press their noses to a yellow square. Then the caller returns the slips to the appropriate bowls, picks 1 from each again, and so on and so on.

[4] Once you've got a body part on a square, it has to stay stuck there. If you unstick yourself, slip, fall, foam at the mouth, bite or lick another player, or make a face that makes a child cry, you're disqualified. The player who lasts the longest in the game wins.

blue

green

soda bottle bowling

Soda Bottle Bowling will put the fizz back in a day that's gone flat. Rummage through the recycling bin for supplies, and in no time you've transformed the hallway into your very own bowling lane.

You will need:

10 plastic soda bottles, each 1 liter, cleaned and dried

Assorted decorating supplies: paint, glitter, glue, beads, construction paper, stickers, or whatever you like (optional)

Funnel

10 cups rice, beans, or sand

Ball, 12 inches in circumference or so (you could also use a ball of yarn)

Paper and pen

[1] Decorate your soda bottles any way you like. If you're a Lady of the Lanes, coat them with glitter and rhinestones. If you're a Bowling Betty, paint them with classic red stripes. Paint faces on them or affix stickers, ribbons, shapes you've cut from construction paper, or whatever you like. Allow everything to set and dry. Or skip the decorations altogether and get right to the action.

[2] Use a funnel to fill each bottle with 1 cup of rice, beans, or sand. Get your ball and take a couple test rolls. If the pins knock over too easily, add more rice. If they don't knock over easily enough, remove some rice.

[3] Set up your bottle bowling pins: five in the back row, then three, then two, then one pin in front.

[4] With your paper and pen, make a score sheet, or photocopy and enlarge the one on the next page.

[5] Step back a few yards and you're ready to roll.

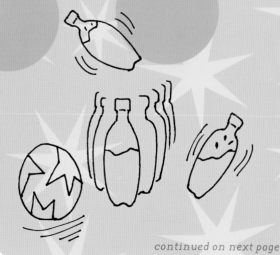

continued on next page

SODA BOTTLE BOWLING LEAGUE CHAMPIONSHIPS

NAME:

Rules

Players take turns trying to knock down the pins. Each player gets to roll twice per turn. You get one point for each pin you knock down. If you knock all the pins down at once, that's a strike. If you knock them all down in two rolls, that's a spare. Either of these stupendous achievements is worthy of a special prize.

Official scoring is pretty tricky. If you are a bowling maven, it is worth learning all the rules regarding strikes and spares (you can use the official scoresheet above). But as a Crafty Girl, your time may be better spent making the world a fun and funky place. Feel free to skip the official league rules and make up your own (we do). Some Crafty Girls we know award a chocolate bar every time all ten pins are knocked down. Others reward gutter balls (balls that hit nothing) with sour candies. Play loud music and develop unusual bowling techniques. It's your thing—do what you want to do. At the end of the game, tally up everyone's points. Whoever has the highest score wins, and must celebrate by doing a funky lane dance.

crafty

scavenger hunt

Sure, scavenger hunts are fun, but for a Crafty Girl like you, they're just not challenging enough. You need a Crafty Scavenger Hunt. Not only do you have to find things, you have to make things. The clock is ticking, your heart is racing, and you're flying through the neighborhood with a basket of freshly completed crafts under your arm. Who said crafting isn't a full-contact sport?

You will need:

Computer and printer OR pen, paper, and a photocopier

Crafty friends

Indulgent neighbors

A prize for the winning team

[1] First make up your Crafty Scavenger Hunt challenge list. Here are some ideas to get you started:
- Make a painting from condiments.
- Make a dress from a trash bag.
- Make a ring from a bag twist-tie.
- Make a frame from a cereal box.
- Make a purse from a margarine tub.

continued on next page

- Make spectacles from pipe cleaners.
- Make sandals from cardboard and string.
- Make a tiara from aluminum foil.
- Make a mask from a paper plate and string.
- Make a hat from an oatmeal canister.
- Make a dog-sized fez from a paper cup.
- Make a wig from yarn or cottonballs.
- Make a flower from a tissue.
- Make an anklet from flowers.
- Make a boat from a milk carton.
- Make a bug out of chewing gum (unchewed, please).
- Make a puppet from a plastic glove.
- Make a necklace from cereal and thread.
- Make a bracelet from candy wrappers.
- Make a lei from crepe paper.

Print or photocopy a copy of the list for each player.

[2] Now you're ready to play. Begin by splitting into teams. Give each player a copy of the challenge list, and you're on your way.

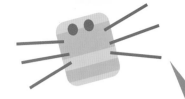

[3] Each team must gather all the materials and make all the crafts. You can conduct the hunt indoors or scour the neighborhood. Players can be fashioning their crafts while scavenging.

[4] When done, the team reports back to the starting point.

[5] The team that finishes first wins the prize and the undying admiration of the whole block.

autobiographical
board games

You've got some free time, a piece of posterboard, and dice. Why not make a board game? You could design a Monopoly-type game based on your block or your school. You could make a game about your favorite hobby, be it soccer or sandwiches. It could be more personal, for instance being called "Get to Know Me," where players could advance only by answering questions about you. Or by paying you compliments. It's your game: you get to make up the rules, and if one of the rules is that other players have to bring you bonbons, then so be it. Here are some ideas for a basic board game to adapt any way you like.

You will need:

Markers

16-by-20-inch piece of posterboard (or borrow a board from a game you already have)

Assorted decorating supplies: stickers, glitter, paint, pictures, or whatever you'd like

20 pieces of cardstock, each 2 by 3 inches

8½-by-11-inch piece of paper

Dice

[1] Draw your game board onto the posterboard. The game should consist of consecutive squares (you'll want at least 30) that can be strung together in any shape you like: a square, a snake, a figure eight, an ice cream cone, or your profile. Decorate with stickers, glitter, paint, pictures, or whatever you'd like. Otherwise, just borrow a board from a game you already have.

[2] Write directions on the squares, like "Skip a turn," "Roll again," etc. If you're using a board borrowed from a store-bought game, just write your directions on blank Post-its and stick them to the existing squares. Get as creative as you'd like. Some examples:

- "Wear a shower cap until you roll a six."
- "Go back 2 squares and suck a lemon for 5 minutes."
- "Eat all the chocolate you can until your next turn."
- "Do the Hokey-Pokey until you roll a four."
- "Wear your socks on your hands until someone else rolls a two."
- "Advance 3 squares and pay the hostess a compliment."
- "Pretend you're the age of the number you just rolled until your next turn."

On several squares, write, "Take a Question Card."

continued on next page

[3] Next, make your Question Cards by writing a question on each piece of cardstock. If your game is all about you, your questions might include the following:

- "What is my most appealing quality?"
- "Which beautiful superstar do I most resemble?"
- "When is my birthday, and what present do you plan to give me?"
- "Which adjective describes me best: 'sparkling,' 'bubbly,' or 'radiant'?"

At the bottom of each card, add a reward and a penalty for getting the answer right or wrong. Some examples:

- "Advance 2 squares for answering correctly; go back 2 and moo like a cow for answering incorrectly."
- "Advance 1 square and pet the cat for answering correctly; go back 1 and pet the lizard for answering incorrectly."
- "Advance to the kitchen and fetch me a lemonade with lots of ice, as neither a right nor a wrong answer is any help in quenching my thirst."

Then make your answer key on the 8½-by-11-inch piece of paper. Entrust the answer key to someone who's not playing the game, and have him or her verify right or wrong answers when question cards are drawn.

[4] Play by rolling dice and following the directions on each square as you land on them. The player who gets to the end first wins—unless, of course, one of the rules is that you win every time no matter what.

What is my most appealing quality?

Which beautiful superstar do I most resemble?

fantasy fort

Sofa cushions and blankets were fine when you were younger, but now you want a more sophisticated fort. This one looks like the inside of a genie's bottle. So fold your arms, blink, nod, and work that ponytail. Your Fantasy Fort wish is our command.

You will need:

5-foot length of PVC tubing, 2 to 3 inches in diameter (available at hardware stores), OR a 5-foot pole, OR, failing all else, 2 cardboard tubes from wrapping paper rolls (the sturdier, the better), each 30 inches long, taped securely together end to end (5-foot total length)

Wrapping paper

Clear tape

Dinner plate

Duct tape

Pretty rocks or crystals

4 pretty color-coordinated sheets, queen size or larger

Needle and thread OR 50 safety pins

Throw pillows

Scarves

Flashlights

Small tape player or CD player and belly dance music

Refreshments

[1] Your PVC tubing, pole, or cardboard will form a tent pole, but before it does, you need to gussy it up. Wrap it in some pretty wrapping paper and secure with clear tape.

[2] Next you'll need to construct a base to keep your tent pole upright. Stand the pole on top of a dinner plate. Make sure it's straight, then secure in place with lots and lots of duct tape. Conceal the tape by spreading pretty rocks or crystals around the plate (this will also help anchor the tent pole in place).

[3] Now you'll make the top by joining your four sheets together to form one giant square. You can baste them together with needle and thread or, if you're a clumsy seamstress, just safety-pin them together as artfully as you can. Drape the giant sheet square over the tent pole to make a teepee.

continued on next page

[4] Work your interior decorating magic. Strew throw pillows and pretty scarves on the floor. Light your fort with flashlights placed near the tent pole. Do not use candles (we know: they're so pretty—but so dangerous, so ix-nay on the andles-cay).

[5] An important part of genie tradition is hospitality, so invite Aladdin, Jasmine, and the rest of your friends over. Entertain them with belly dance music and serve meze platters of snacks, like hummus and pita and halvah and peach juice. You're rocking the Casbah, all right.

fortune-telling

fun

Once you've got your Fantasy Fort established, why not set up shop as a fortune-teller? There are many methods of fortune-telling: horoscopes, tarot cards, crystal balls, cootie catchers, divination pendulums, and palm-reading. We prefer fortune cookies and tea leaves, because they predict the future and provide a tasty snack. Make a batch of the delicious Funny Fortune Cookies on page 117 to hand out to fort visitors with tea. Read the Oracle Board while they nosh. We see crafty fun in your future.

Tasseomancy Tea

You will need:

1 cup water

1 tablespoon loose tea leaves

A simple, light-colored cup

[1] With adult supervision, bring water to a boil. While the water is bubbling, dump the tea leaves into your empty cup.

[2] Pour boiling water over tea leaves. Allow to steep and cool for 5 minutes or so. When the tea is cool enough, drink up. Savor. Relax.

continued on next page

[3] When there's only a teaspoon or two of tea left, swirl the tea around while concentrating on something in the future you're curious about. When the leaves settle down, look in your cup. What you see is your fortune. If you were wondering what you would get for your birthday and you see a pony shape in the tea leaves, you're a very fortunate girl.

Makes 1 cup.

Oracle Board

You will need:

Markers

12-by-12-inch piece of posterboard

Assorted decorating supplies: stickers, glitter, rhinestones, glue, paint, or whatever you'd like

Single die

[1] Draw a grid on your posterboard, 4 squares by 4 squares, for a total of 16 squares.

[2] In each square write a different category and six choices. Some examples:

PET	CITY	# OF KIDS	JOB
1. Horse	1. Honolulu	1. 12	1. Car mechanic
2. Iguana	2. Peoria	2. 3	2. Ice cream taster
3. Platypus	3. Cairo	3. 0	3. Marine biologist
4. Hairless cat	4. St. Petersburg	4. 6	4. Secretary of state
5. Tarantula	5. Hong Kong	5. 2	5. Fish psychologist
6. Teacup poodle	6. Juneau	6. 38	6. CIA operative

[3] Decorate your board with glitter, rhinestones, stickers, or whatever you'd like.

[4] To play, roll a die onto the board grid. The die predicts the choice for whatever square it lands on. So, if your die ends up on the PET square and you have rolled a five, this means you'll be the proud owner of a tarantula. Lucky you.

pet   city   kids   job

cryptology
crafts

Passing notes is an art, indeed a craft. A Crafty Girl like you won't settle for ragged three-hole, ruled paper and chicken scratch. Your notes are masterpieces. More importantly, they are snoop-proof, artfully concealing their secrets. These projects will ensure your notes say nothing if they fall into the wrong hands.

Swiss Cheese Decoder Key

A Swiss Cheese Decoder Key makes sense of a scrambled letter. Give one to your most trusted confidant.

You will need:

Small, pointy scissors, such as manicure or embroidery scissors

2 or more pieces of paper, each 8½ by 11 inches

Paper clips (optional)

Pen

[1] Using your small scissors, cut 30 or so word-sized holes (about 1 inch long by ¼ inch high) all over a page. When you're done, the page should look like Swiss cheese. If you have partners in crime, you'll want to make identical decoders, one for each of you. It's easiest to place two or more sheets together, secure with paper clips so they stay precisely aligned, and cut your message holes through both at once. Use them over and over. They'll never get the goods on you, shady lady.

[2] To use, place this Swiss Cheese Decoder over the blank piece of paper and write your message through the holes. Remove the decoder and write random words all over the rest of the message page. Your letter will look like nonsense by itself, but when you place the decoder over it, the message emerges.

Invisible Ink

Do we have to spell it out for you? If you have top secret information to pass on, you need invisible ink.

You will need:

8½-by-11-inch piece of paper

Toothpick

2 tablespoons lemon juice

Iron

continued on next page

[1] Tear the edges of your paper to give it an old, parchmenty look.

[2] Write your message on your paper, using a toothpick dipped in lemon juice as pen and ink. Don't use too much, or the paper will warp. When it dries, your message will be invisible.

[3] To read your letter, run an iron over the paper. Remember: paper + hot iron = fire, so don't leave the iron on long enough to singe, and do make sure an adult is present. The heat will make the writing appear.

Jigsaw Letter

As a covert operator, you're hard to read, and your letters are, too. This letter reveals itself when the recipient solves the puzzle.

You will need:

Marker

8-by-10-inch piece of posterboard

Pencil

Scissors

Envelope

[1] Write your message in marker on the posterboard.

[2] In pencil, draw interlocking, puzzle-shaped pieces all over the posterboard.

[3] Cut out pieces along pencil lines.

[4] Put pieces into an envelope and send to a trusted confidant. For extra security send the pieces in several different envelopes.

Variation

A picture says a thousand words. Instead of writing a letter, you could glue a color copy of a photo to the posterboard, then cut into puzzle pieces.

fill in
the blanks

98

> *Fill in the Blanks are like Mad Libs gone completely insane. Take a passage from your favorite book, blank out the key words, and fill in the fun. Cut loose Crafty Girl–style and learn a little grammar while you do.*

You will need:

Books, magazines, pamphlets, or other written material

A computer and printer

Construction paper

Stapler or brads

[1] First you'll need to find some funny passages to use. Flip through your favorite books and magazines. Skim pamphlets, papers, even cereal boxes. Peruse the yearbook, the school bulletin, or homework assignments. You never know what will provide great Fill in the Blank material. (The funniest one we ever did came from a biography of the New Kids on the Block. Go figure.) Find at least 10 good passages, each one paragraph long.

[2] Type up your passages on the computer. Then go back and delete some words, replacing each with an apt description or naming the part of speech, in caps. So if you delete "Shakespeare," you'll replace it with "FAMOUS WRITER." If you delete "write," you'll replace it with "VERB." If you delete "Alas!" you'll replace it with "EXCLAMATION." And so on. Delete at least 10 words per passage and be sure to leave a blank space before each description, so you can write something in later.

[3] Print out your passages. Make a pretty cover from construction paper and bind the whole thing together with staples or brads.

[4] To play, ask your friends to name a FAMOUS WRITER, a VERB, an EXCLAMATION—whatever the descriptive capitals call for. Write down their suggestions in the blanks, then read the whole passage aloud. "EDGAR ALLAN POE dressed himself in his favorite DISCO HOT PANTS. He was eager to go ROLLER-SKATE. On his way, he noticed his chambermaid had DROOLED upon his master-piece. 'DON'T GO THERE, GIRL!' he exclaimed." Bah hah hah hah hah.

Chapter 4

gifts to make
and goodies to bake

fancy stationery kit

E-mail and phone messages are great, but they can't compare to the feeling of seeing a letter in the mailbox, especially if it's decorated by hand. It's easy to design your own stationery, either for a special gift or as your trademark letterhead. Right on, write now.

You will need:

6 sheets of pretty paper

Glue

Assorted decorating supplies: ribbon, rickrack, rubber stamps, colored pens, metallic pens, stencils, paints, crayons, pressed flowers, whatever

Ruler

6 envelopes

Plain stickers

Pencil

Scissors

8½-by-11-inch sheet of card stock (stiff enough to be used for postcards)

10-inch piece of ribbon

[1] Decorate the six pieces of pretty paper. Don't forget to leave room for the letter part.
Some cool ideas to try:

- Glue on a ribbon border.
- Rubber-stamp a pattern.
- Draw a flowering vine.
- Draw colored lines with a ruler for the text of the letter.
- Create a monogram using calligraphy.
- Make curlicues with a gold or silver pen.
- Glue on pressed flowers.

[2] Decorate the envelopes to match.

[3] Decorate the stickers with hearts, flowers, drawings, slogans (*Hola chica! Ciao bella! Par Avion, Special Delivery, You're a star!*), or whatever.

[4] Using ruler, pencil, and scissors, measure and cut card stock in quarters (each 4 1/4 by 5 1/2 inches). On one side, draw lines for the "to" and "from" addresses and a box for the stamp. On the other side, decorate around the edges, leaving room in the middle for a short letter.

[5] Assemble the paper, envelopes, stickers, and postcards as a packet and tie with the ribbon.

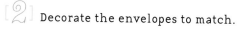

greeting card

Thinking of that someone special? Make him or her a mini-masterpiece to say thank you, I miss you, or happy birthday.

You will need:

8½-by-11-inch sheet of card stock (stiff paper)

Ruler

Scissors

X-acto knife (caution: X-acto blades are sharp—ask an adult to help) and self-healing mat or newspaper (optional)

Glue

Photographs (silly ones are ideal) or magazines or newspapers to cut up for collage

Assorted decorating supplies: ribbon, rick-rack, glitter, rubber stamps, stickers, fancy pens, paints, whatever

[1] Fold card stock in half to make a card.

[2] Using ruler and scissors, cut out a 2-by-3-inch window in front. The X-acto knife makes it much easier.

[3] Glue a photograph or magazine or newspaper picture to backside of front so you can see it through the window when the card is closed.

[4] Decorate the window frame however you like. Add the beginning of a message, such as *There's only one thing I have to say . . .* or *I was just thinking . . .*

[5] Inside, complete the message (*Happy Birthday! Thank You! You're the best! Friends are forever!*). Decorate the inside like a maniac.

sachet

Drifting off to sleep with the fragrance of rose petals or lavender practically guarantees a night of sweet dreams. This easy sachet will make your bedroom or closet smell like heaven. It also makes a pretty present.

You will need:

12-inch length of velvet ribbon, 3 inches wide

Clear nail polish

Straight pins

Needle and thread

Potpourri, rose petals, or lavender flowers
(approximately 1½ cups)

[1] Seal ends of ribbon with clear nail polish to prevent fraying.

[2] Fold ribbon in half so it measures 6 by 3 inches. Make sure that velvety side faces in. Pin sides together.

[3] Stitch long sides together, leaving ¼-inch seam allowance. Stop stitching ½ inch from end on both sides.

[4] Turn inside out. Fill with potpourri, rose petals, or lavender flowers.

[5] Fold in ½ inch of fabric along top edge. Pin together and sew shut. Breathe deeply. Ahhhhh.

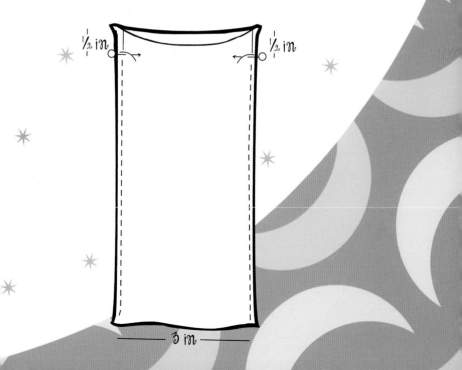

½ in   ½ in

3 in

bath
biscuits

Biscuits for the bathtub? Why yes, my skeptical little friend. Toss a couple of these fragrant cookies into a hot bath and let the good times roll. They fizz, they make the water soft and sweet, they smell great, and they come in fun shapes and colors.

You will need:

2 cups fine sea salt

$\frac{1}{2}$ cup cornstarch, plus a little extra for rolling out dough

$\frac{1}{2}$ cup baking soda

2 eggs

2 tablespoons vegetable oil

1 teaspoon vitamin E oil (if you can't find the liquid, break open some capsules)

5 to 10 drops essential oil or perfume oil in your favorite scent

1 tablespoon dried, chopped lavender, rosemary, or sage (optional)

Food dye (optional)

Rolling pin

Cookie cutters (or use a sturdy glass tumbler to cut rounds)

[1] In a large mixing bowl, stir together sea salt, cornstarch, baking soda, eggs, oil, vitamin E oil, essential oil, and herbs, if using, until the mixture forms a dough. If you want to make biscuits in various colors, separate the dough into three or four balls, add a few drops of food dye to each, and knead until blended.

[2] Dust rolling pin and cutting board or table with extra cornstarch and roll out dough 3/4-inch thick. Cut into fun shapes with cookie cutters, use the opening of a glass to make rounds, or roll dough into little life preservers.

[3] Place 1 inch apart on an ungreased cookie sheet. Bake at 350 degrees for 10 to 12 minutes. Allow to cool.

[4] Store biscuits in a cool, dry place. To use, run a bath, toss a biscuit or two into the water, and enjoy.

Makes about 16 biscuits.

critter-in-the-middle
soap treats

Like prehistoric ants trapped in amber, plastic bugs or fig-urines float magically inside these bars of translucent soap. Feature your favorite creatures or try plastic hearts, stars, aliens, nuns, hula dancers, babies, dinosaurs, or any other tiny treasures that will stand up to heat, soap, and water.

You will need:

16 ounces glycerin soap base (look for it at craft stores, along with other soap-making supplies—if you can't find any, just use a transparent soap like Neutrogena)

5 to 10 drops perfume or essential oil, such as lavender, vanilla, or eucalyptus, for adding a delicious fragrance (optional)

Soap molds (buy them at a craft store or improvise with available kitchen supplies; ice cube trays work well, and you can also use glasses, Pyrex cups, or ceramic ramekins—almost anything will work, as long as it's not aluminum, which reacts with the lye in soaps)

Petroleum jelly or vegetable shortening

Small plastic creatures or whatever you plan to trap in your soap

Wax paper

[1] Get an adult to help you chop up the soap into small chunks.

[2] In a medium-size, microwave-safe mixing bowl, melt the soap base in microwave on high in 1-minute intervals.

[3] Add perfume oil, if using.

[4] Grease soap molds with petroleum jelly or vegetable shortening. Carefully pour the melted soap base into the molds until they are filled halfway. Allow to cool for five or ten minutes, then place plastic creatures on top. Pour the rest of the soap base over the creatures, until the molds are full.

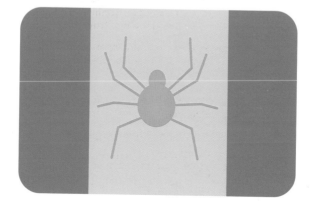

111

continued on next page

[5] Cool thoroughly, then release from molds. Soap shrinks as it cools, so you shouldn't have any problem getting your soaps loose, but if you do, carefully jimmy them free with a butter knife. Wrap with wax paper and store in a cool, dry place.

Makes about 4 bars, depending on size of molds.

Flower Power Soap Variation

Instead of a plastic critter, float a silk or plastic flower inside your soap. Add a floral essential oil to make it smell as pretty as it looks. You can also add soap colorant (available at craft stores) to tint your soap a blossoming shade of pink, purple, or yellow.

kitchen sink
cookies

Sure, chocolate chip cookies are tasty, but they're not very exciting. These cookies incorporate everything but the kitchen sink. How's that for excitement? You'll need an adult on hand to supervise the oven proceedings.

You will need:

1 cup butter or margarine

½ cup brown sugar

½ cup white sugar

1 egg, beaten

¾ teaspoon vanilla extract

1 cup flour

½ teaspoon salt

½ teaspoon baking soda

1½ to 2 cups of add-ins: candy, nuts, oatmeal, peanut butter, or whatever you like

1 Preheat oven to 375 degrees F. In a large bowl, cream together butter or margarine, brown sugar, and white sugar. When the mixture is well blended, add egg and vanilla.

continued on next page

[2] In a separate bowl, combine flour, salt, and baking soda. Mix well. Add flour mixture to butter mixture and stir until well-blended.

[3] Stir in your add-ins. Experiment. How do licorice bits, pine nuts, and peanut butter taste together? What about cinnamon, white chocolate chips, and caramel? Sun-dried tomato, banana chips, and wheat germ? Bear in mind that you might want to eat these, though, so don't let your combinations get too gross, unless you have a dog to eat the rejects.

[4] Drop spoonfuls of dough on a cookie sheet, 1 inch apart. Bake for 8 to 10 minutes. Transfer to a rack to cool.

Makes about 3 dozen cookies.

blueberry chip cookie

lemon lime swirl cookie

orange creamy dream cookie

invent your own
ice cream

You scream for ice cream, but you want something more exotic than vanilla. Perhaps Prune-Papaya Passion is more your speed, or maybe you're nuts for Goober Grape-nut. Shake up some ice cream with resealable bags, ice, and rock salt and invent your own taste sensation.

You will need:

1 gallon-size resealable plastic bag

8 cups ice

⅓ cup rock salt

1 quart-size resealable plastic bag

1 cup whole milk or half-and-half (or a combination of the two)

3 tablespoons sugar

¼ teaspoon vanilla

Clean, dry pint-sized ice cream container

½ cup add-ins: candy, nuts, cereal, cookies, marshmallows, chocolate chunks, or whatever you like

9-by-12-inch piece of construction paper

Scissors

Markers

Clear tape

continued on next page

[1] Fill larger plastic bag with ice. Add rock salt.

[2] Fill smaller plastic bag with milk or half-and-half, sugar, and vanilla. Seal well.

[3] Place the smaller plastic bag inside the larger plastic bag. Seal well. Shake until the mixture turns into ice cream (about 5 minutes).

[4] Transfer your ice cream to your container and stir in your add-ins. Be creative. Try peanut butter, marshmallow fluff, and graham crackers. How about pretzels, peanuts, and chocolate chips; toffee bits, caramel, and cashews; jam and chocolate chunks and dried cranberries; or anything you think you might want to eat.

[5] Come up with a name for your creation. Then make a label from construction paper. Cut paper into two pieces: a circle ($3\frac{1}{2}$ inches in diameter) for the top; and a trapezoid (4 inches wide, 12 inches long at the top, but 11 inches long at the bottom) for the side. Decorate label however you'd like and attach to container with clear tape. Store ice cream in freezer until you're ready to eat it.

Makes about 2 cups.

Instant Gratification Variation

If you don't have time to Invent Your Own Ice Cream, you can use store-bought vanilla (or whatever flavor you like) and just mix in your custom add-ins.

116

funny
fortune cookies

117

Aren't fortune cookies the best? They provide a taste treat and dispense wisdom. Make a batch yourself, and you can customize your cookies with kooky fortunes. You'll need an adult to supervise the hot cookie handling. Then chow down. Crafty Girl Says: good snacking brings good fortune.

You will need:

Pen

20 strips of paper, ½ inch wide and 2 inches long

1 cup flour

½ cup sugar

2 tablespoons cornstarch

⅓ cup oil

3 egg whites

¼ cup water

¾ teaspoon vanilla

Aluminum foil

Nonstick cooking spray

Your true love will look like a r

Your lucky number is 2

continued on next page

Your true love will have double-jointe~ ... like in a bowl of Alpha-Bits

You will discover tr~

An albino hamster will bring yo~

[1] Write fortunes on the 20 slips of paper. Make them
as funny, crazy, or cryptic as you'd like.

[2] Preheat oven to 300 degrees F. In a large bowl,
combine flour, sugar, and cornstarch. Add
oil, egg whites, water, and vanilla and mix
until well blended.

[3] Line a baking sheet with aluminum foil.
Spray foil with nonstick cooking spray.
Then drop teaspoons of batter onto the foil,
5 inches apart. With a spoon, spread each
glob of batter into a 4-inch circle.

An act of kindness will be repaid in a thousand c~ ~y bars

The family pet loves you best

[4] Bake for 15 to 20 minutes, until the cookies just start to brown. Then get ready to work quickly, because the cookies harden 15 seconds after they come out of the oven.

[5] Remove one cookie from the oven with a spatula. Place a fortune in the center and fold cookie in half. Then fold again so the points touch to make a fortune cookie-shape. You may need to press the cookie against the kitchen counter to get it to bend. Don't press too hard, though, or the cookie will break. Place completed cookie in a muffin tin to cool. Repeat with the rest of the batter.

Makes 20 cookies

You will wear your Wednesday underwear on

u will make your fortune from granola bars

Bananas for breakfast will o, if you lick all day

Your secret admirer wears green shoes

the end